What Can Fox Play?

by Amy Jo • illustrated by Holly Clifton Brown

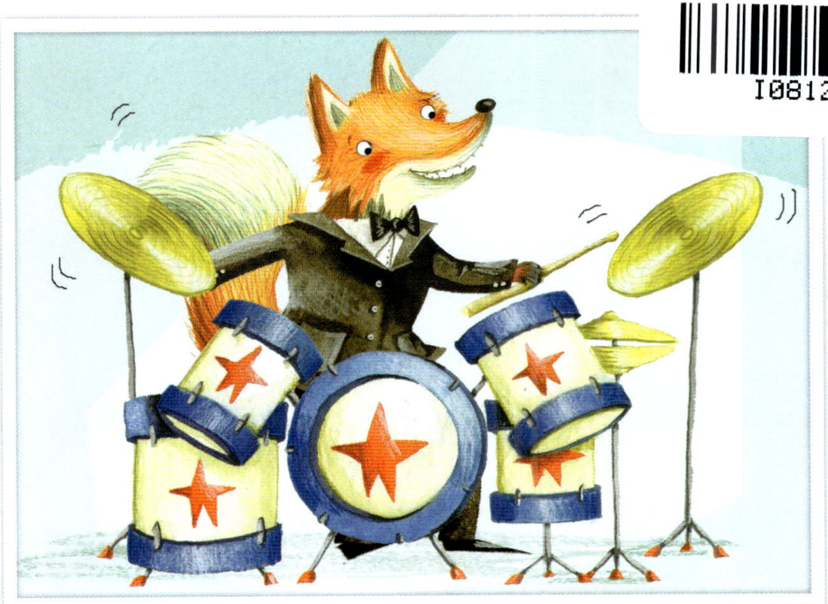

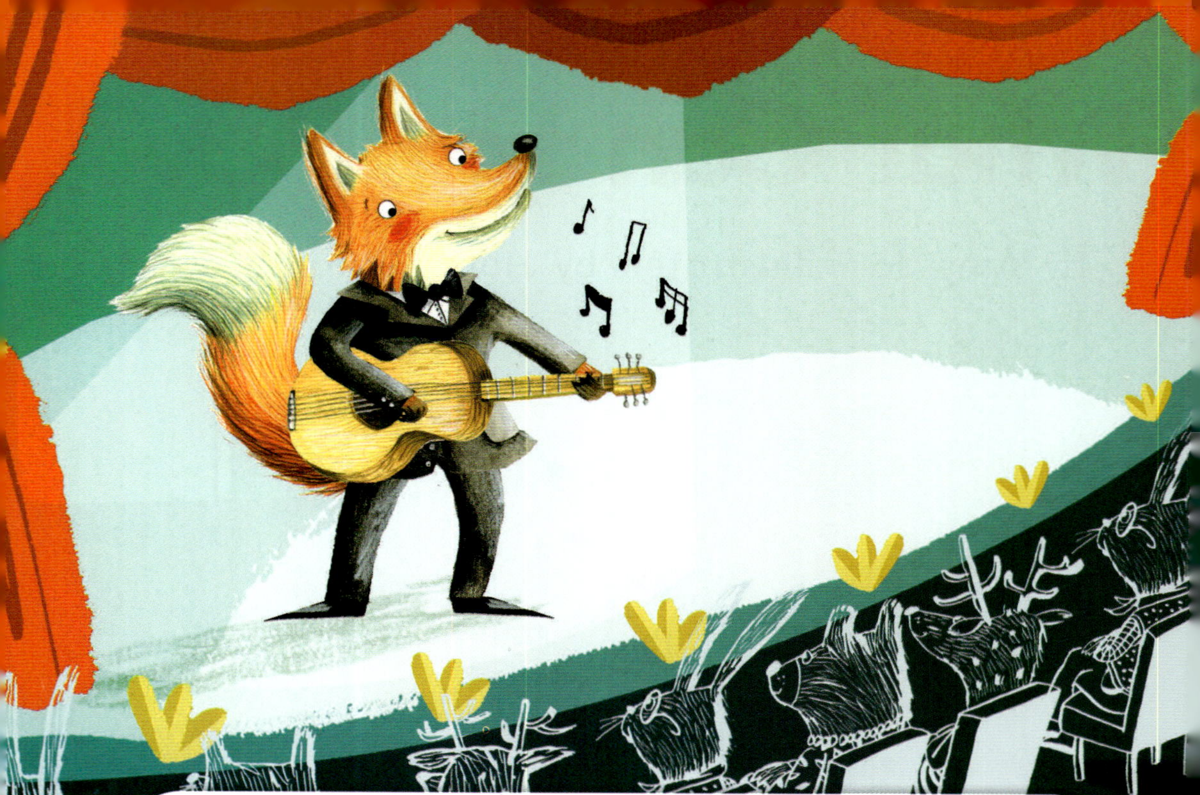

Fox can play the 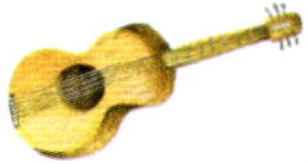 guitar.

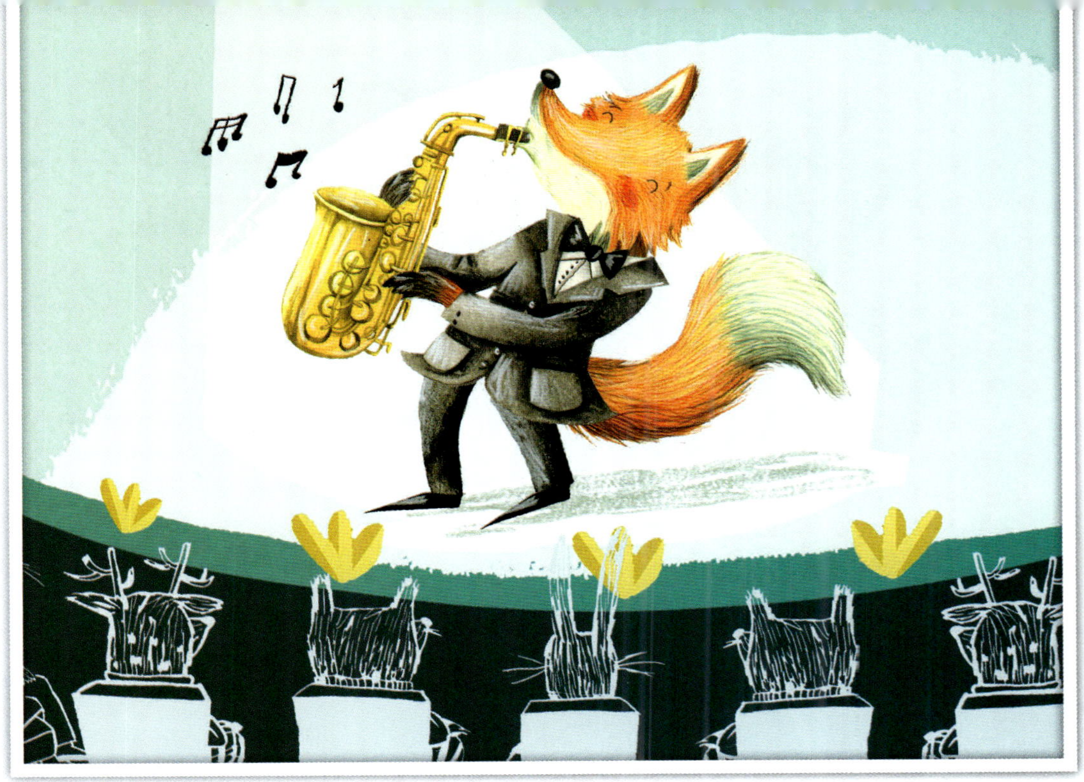

Fox can play the sax.

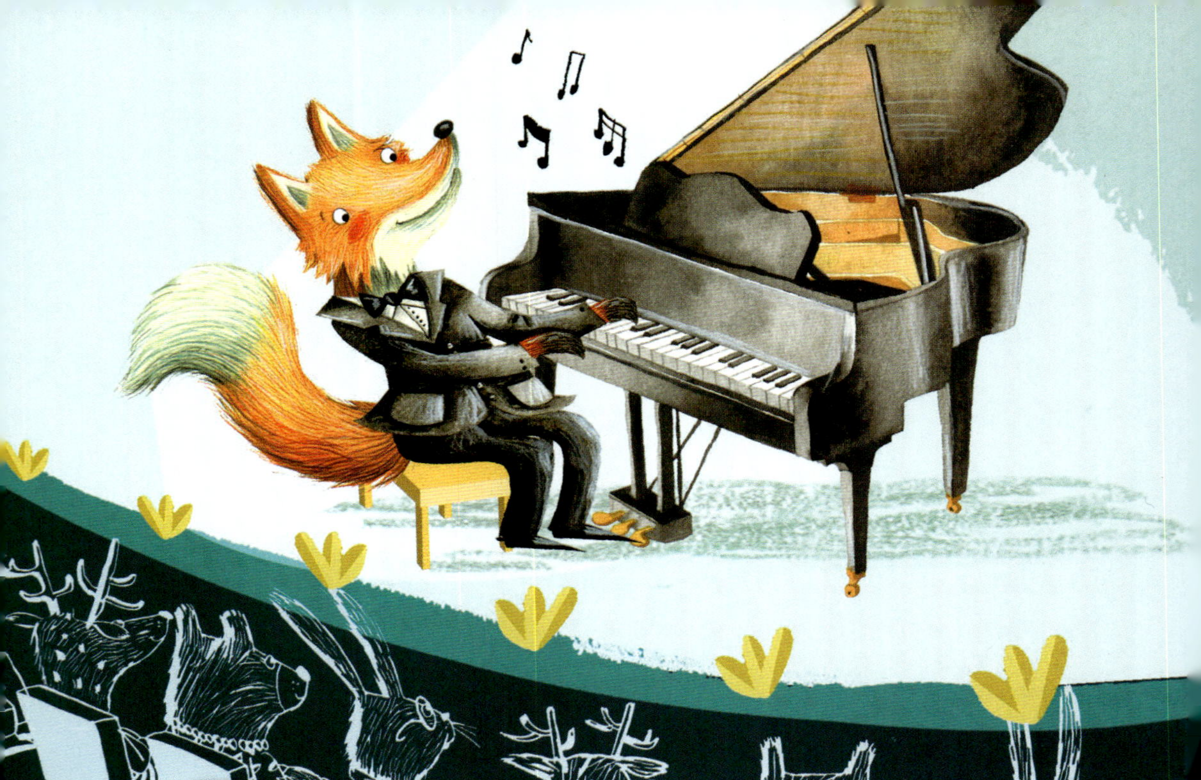

Fox can play the 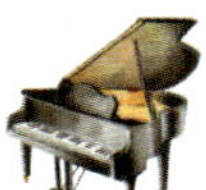 piano .

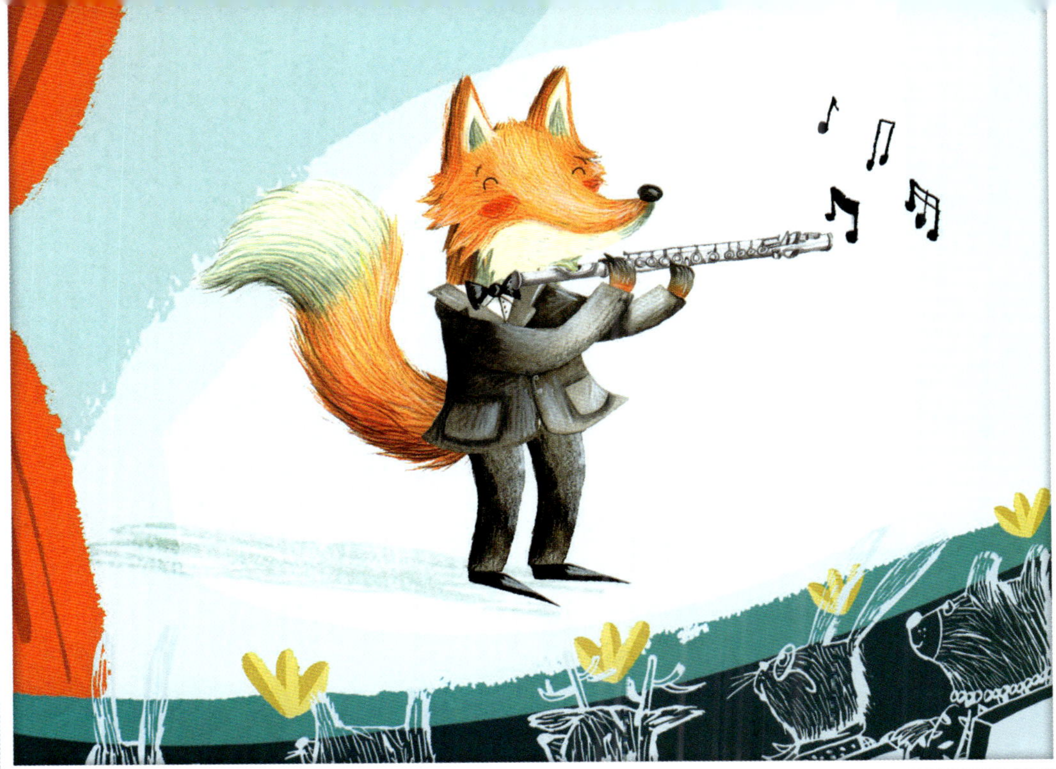

Fox can play the 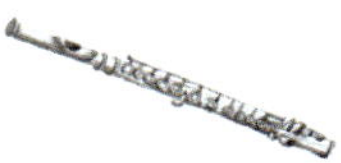 flute .

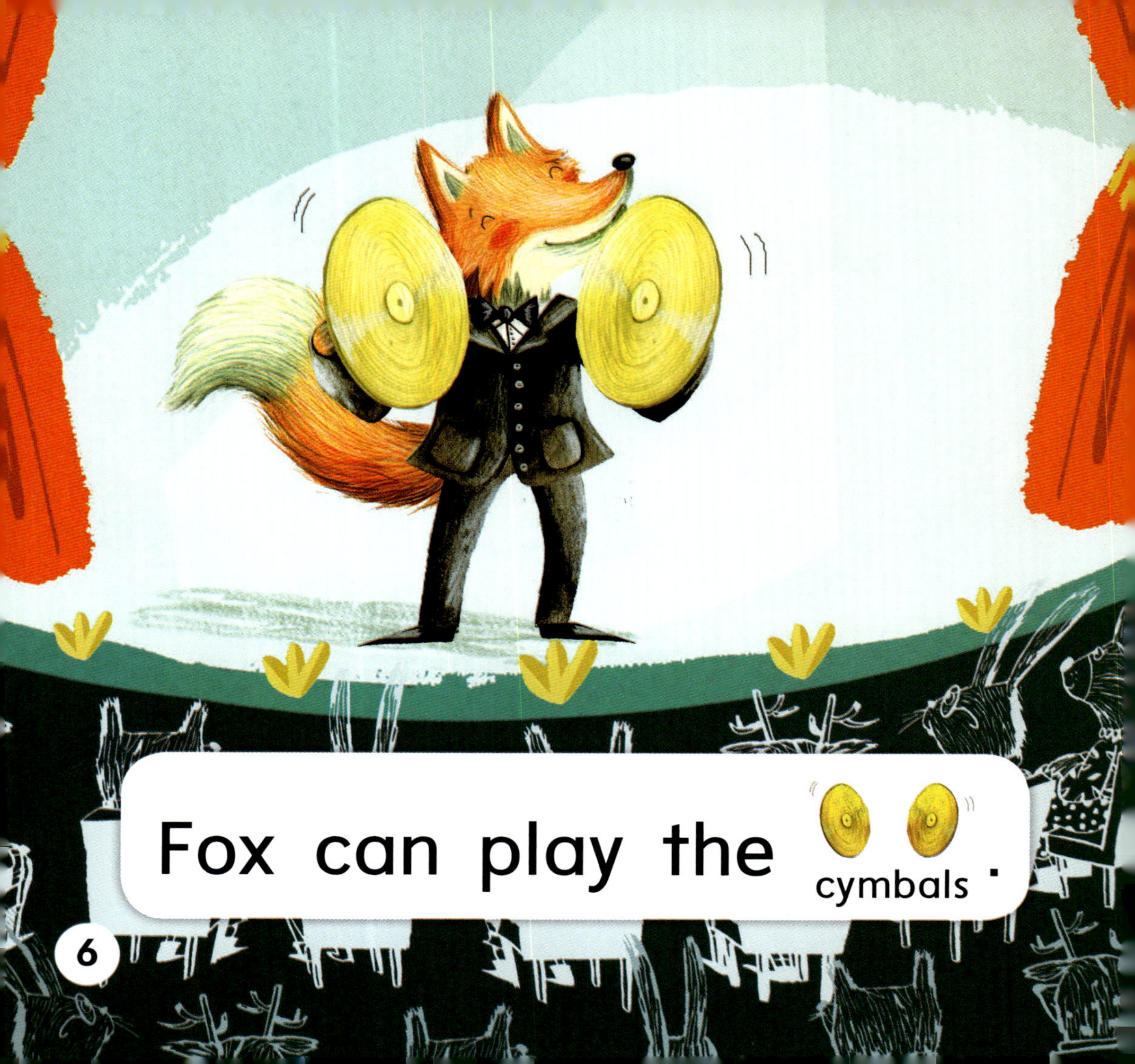

Fox can play the cymbals .

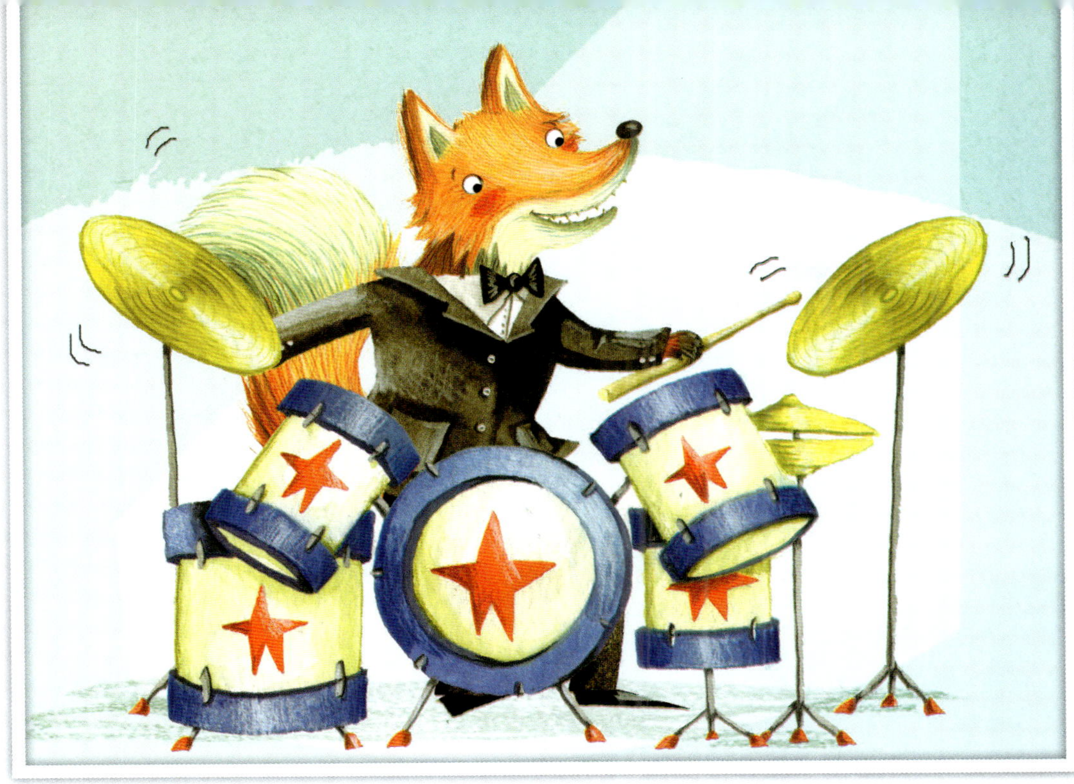

Fox can play the 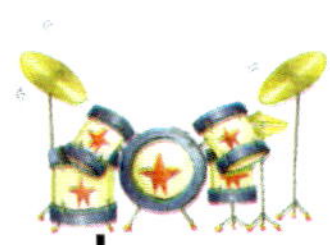 drums .

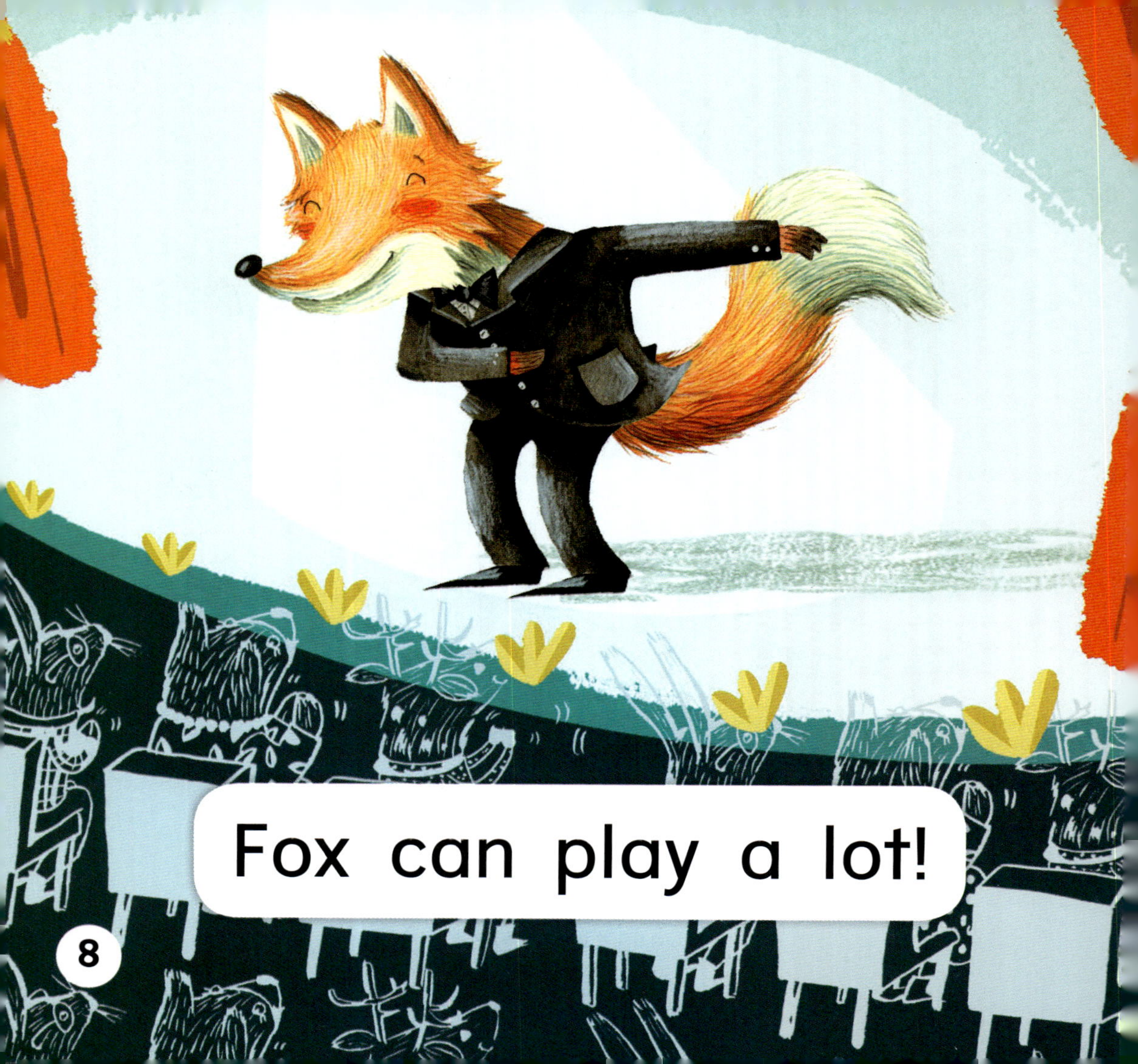

Fox can play a lot!